TRENTHAM
THROUGH TIME
Alan Myatt

AMBERLEY

Acknowledgements

My thanks must go to David Cooke who has been a good friend for forty years and has collected images of Trentham all his life. He has allowed me free access to his collection, and for this I am truly grateful. Thanks to Dave Hissey of Turbine Garage who immediately downed tools to show me around his premises. I must also thank Newcastle Borough Museum and Art Gallery for the use of the photograph of skaters on Trentham Lake. All the staff at Stoke-on-Trent Archives, where most of my research took place. Liz Weaver for the photograph of James Edwards, and thanks to Amberley Publishing who thought the project was worthwhile. Thanks to Kath Peake for her hospitality and enabling me to photograph the Crown Devon Plaques with Trentham hunting dogs. Many images are from my own postcard collection, but some are from a time before photography so an engraving has had to suffice. As far as I am aware, I have used only one copyright image. If I have inadvertently used others without permission I can only apologise.

First published 2015

Amberley Publishing
The Hill, Stroud, Gloucestershire, GL5 4EP
www.amberley-books.com

Copyright © Alan Myatt, 2015

The right of Alan Myatt to be identified as the
Author of this work has been asserted in accordance with
the Copyrights, Designs and Patents Act 1988.

ISBN 978 1 4456 4702 9 (print)
ISBN 978 1 4456 4703 6 (ebook)

British Library Cataloguing in Publication Data.
A catalogue record for this book is available from the
British Library.

Typesetting by Amberley Publishing.
Printed in Great Britain.

Introduction

Trentham's sylvan landscape at the head of the Vale of Trent owes its existence to the river that runs through it. The source of the Trent is high on Biddulph Moor, where it trickles from a spout with a stone above dated 1935.

It tiptoes cautiously around the edge of the Potteries before going underground at Stoke. From here it's path ran to the east of Primrose Hill, meandering through the wide valley where the canal and railway now are. During the last Ice Age 20,000 years ago, the valley was blocked by debris left by the retreating ice sheet and the river shifted to the west of Primrose Hill where it still runs. It is the third longest river in Britain and the only one that heads south, before taking fright near Alrewas and rushing north to the Humber. The name 'Trent' is Celtic for trespasser, named so due to the river constantly changing course and flooding the land. It was named 'Trisantona' under the Romans and in the eighth century, 'Treonte'. In the years 1101 and 1581 it is recorded as drying up altogether.

Ancient man would have lived on the high ground and only ventured into the wooden valley, where wolves roamed, to hunt deer and wild boar. There were two burial mounds at Trentham during the Bronze Age; one overlooked the river at the Northwood and another in the park to the west, which is now lost.

Trentham was in the Kingdom of Mercia under pagan King Wulfhere, who had his camp at Bury Bank, which overlooked the important river crossing at Darlaston, near Stone. He killed his two sons in a rage when they converted to Christianity, but his daughter, Werburgh, founded religious houses at Hanbury and Trentham. Granddaughter of the mighty King Penda, she died at Threckingham around 690 and was buried at Hanbury. Her body was removed to Chester in 875 for safety from the Danes, who also attacked Trentham. The nunnery was rebuilt in 907 by Elfleda, daughter of Alfred the Great.

The site was given to Hugh Lupus, 1st Earl of Chester, around 1087. Many religious houses fell into ruin during the unsettled times after the Norman invasion. The foundation charter of Trentham priory, which dedicated it to Saint Mary and All Saints, was given on the deathbed of Ranulph, 4th Earl of Chester, in 1153 and speaks of the restoration of an abbey of cannons. The later priory of Austin Cannons was founded in 1251. Trentham was considered to be one of the wealthier priories, but by 1344 its wealth had been greatly reduced. Henry VIII broke with Rome in 1534 and dissolved Trentham priory in 1537, stripping it of valuables, roof timbers, lead and windows, leaving only the church. The remains were sold to Charles Brandon, 1st Duke of Suffolk, in 1538, who quickly sold it to Thomas Pope. In 1540, Pope sold it on to James Leveson, whose family remained until 1912. The priory's small tower is preserved at Dalbury Lees church in South Derbyshire. Such was the early history of Trentham.

The first mention of a hall is in 1599, incorporating the priory ruins. A new hall was built by Richard Leveson in 1633 using stone from Beech Cliff, redesigned in 1707 for Lord Gower, and again in 1737. The house was much altered between 1775 and 1778 by the 2nd Earl Gower and additions were made in 1814–17. The last house was a ducal palace, built between 1834 and 1839 by the 2nd Duke of Sutherland, around the core of the old hall. This hall was abandoned by the family in 1907 and finally demolished in May 1912, the building material sold off at a fraction of its true value.

Trentham has been home to a saint and several dukes and has seen many important visitors, including a young Victoria, later Queen Victoria. Now it is your turn to tread in the footsteps of kings, nobility and statesmen.

Welcome to Trentham. The gardens were opened to the public on a regular basis from 1910, and by 1925 they were advertising motor launches and rowing boats, a miniature railway and swimming baths. Admission was 1*s* 6*d* with tea at 5*d* a pot. The ballroom was advertised as the largest in the Midlands, which seems strange when all information tells us that it was actually built in 1931. Apparently there had been an earlier ballroom. In 1931, Trentham Gardens Ltd was formed to manage the estate and a painting by George Romney was sold by the Sutherland family to partly fund the new ballroom and swimming baths. In 1981, the estate was sold to John Broome for £3 million, whose great plan included building holiday lodges. His plans were thwarted by subsidence and difficulty with planning permission when authorities thought it had a Disneyland feel about it. It seems John Broome was responsible for removing most things of value from Trentham to fund his other leisure complex at Alton Towers. In 1984, the National Coal Board purchased Trentham and promised to make good any damage causes by subsidence – beginning with draining the lake in 1985. In 1989, the Coal Board put the estate up for sale and it was bought by Saint Modwen in 1996, who reopened it to the public in 2004. It consists of 725 acres with 600 local jobs created and 3 million visitors per year. Plans to refurbish the last remnants of Trentham Hall were put on hold when, in 2013, it was estimated the cost would be £35 million. There were plans to build a five-star hotel on the site of the hall, but these too have been put on hold for the time being. In the meantime, many millions have been spent restoring the gardens to their former glory, mainly thanks to Saint Modwen for their leap of faith. I had intended to write about both Trentham Hall and village, but the hall has such a complex story that it had to take priority. I have not covered the railway, canal or farms; perhaps they might appear in a future volume of *Trentham Through Time*.

Burial Mound

Dating from the Bronze Age, this burial mound was discovered in May 1859 and can be seen in a field overlooking the Trent at the Northwood. Excavations revealed evidence of burning and small sandstone slabs, beneath which lay part of a human skull, thigh bones, vertebrae and ribs with the canine tooth of a dog. The remains of a cinerary urn were also found and are on display at the Potteries Museum. Ploughing is limited to a depth of 6 inches, but bone fragments are still often unearthed.

River Trent

The river has its source marked with a stone dated 1935 on Biddulph Moor, where it trickles from a small pipe and from where Trentham gets its name. In July 1996, half of a Bronze Age sword was found at Primrose Hill, Hanford. It was matched with another half that had been found earlier on the other side of the River Trent in Trentham Park, 3 miles away. Its owner was a nobleman who died around 900 BC. The sword was probably broken on purpose and scattered to kill any power it had.

Princess Werburgh

Werburgh was a royal princess who studied under her aunt Etheldreda, the first abbess of Ely. Werburgh became abbess of Trentham around 679 and founded nunneries at Weedon, Hanbury and Trentham. She died in 699 at Threckingham was buried there, but moved to Hanbury becoming a saint shortly after her death. Her relics were removed in 907 due to the threat from the Danes and taken 80 miles to the abbey of Saint Werburgh at Chester. Her shrine stands behind the high altar at Chester Cathedral.

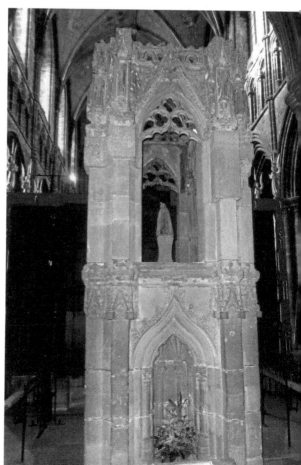

Trentham Priory

The priory was built over the remains of Werburgh's nunnery. Its foundation charter was granted by the Earl of Chester in 1087 to Benedictine monks dedicated to Saint Mary and All Saints and later re-founded to the Augustinians in 1153. It was seized by King Henry in 1537. The lead roof timbers and windows were removed. Other goods listed were a silver chalice, vestments, three bells from the steeple, a cross of copper and gilt, a small brass book, towels and altar cloths, candlesticks and money. The small tower was taken to Dalbury Leese in Derbyshire, being repaired in 2014.

Trentham Church

The nave of the church was the only part of the priory not to be slighted by King Henry due to it being the parish church. By 1762, the tower was found to be unsafe and was taken down. In 1830, the roof and north wall were in a poor state and the church was closed for rebuilding. In 1842, only the south wall facing the new hall was left standing and the Norman pillars were carefully taken down and rebuilt in their original position. The porch, dated 1153, is from a previous building.

Church Bells

These were sold to Saint Margaret's in Wolstanton in 1767, as Trentham's bell tower had been demolished in 1762. The Trentham six are inscribed with Abr Rudhall, 1714; Richard Marlowe William Hall, 1714; Jeffrey Williams, 1714; George Plaxton, 1714; Richard Asburie (blacksmith), 1623; and John and Catherine Gower, 1714. One bell was purchased from Wolstanton and now hangs in the Sutherland Mausoleum. The bells are pictured waiting to be rehung after cleaning in May 1948 at Wolstanton.

Knight's Effigy

This broken figure, dated 1215, is thought to be Earl Randel sitting in a niche on the north aisle and is almost unique, as the knight is holding his helmet close to his chest. It would have originally been the cover to a table monument. It was found among fragments in the churchyard in 1854. In the porch is a stone lid from the grave of a Knight Templar, dated around 1250, that features a Calvary Cross and a sword, which signifies nobility. This was found being used as a drain cover deep below ground.

Praying Cross

This praying or preaching cross, seen being repaired in the churchyard in 1949, has a Saxon base and is said to be the place where Saint Werburgh's body rested overnight on her journey to Chester. Holes can be seen at the top where an upper section would have fitted. The praying stone itself is inscribed on the underside with a Roman spear and is of a later date. Its original site would have been much deeper than the present ground level. It could have been brought from elsewhere by the Leveson Gowers to add a sense of antiquity to the site.

The Elizabethan Hall of Richard Leveson

Built in 1599, the first hall incorporated the priory ruins. The featured Elizabethan hall of Richard Leveson was built in 1633 using stone from the caves at Beech Cliff, built in a H-shape and with large mullion windows for which he employed a man to maintain. There was a large sundial on the wall and a separate bird aviary. The core of the house survived several rebuilds and when the last hall was demolished in 1912, these semis were constructed out of salvaged stone on Northwood Lane, possibly from the Elizabethan hall.

Beech Caves

These were formed using pillar and stall workings in the red-sandstone cliff. Documents show that Roger Low was paid 22*d* a score to remove 130 feet of stone in August 1633 to build Trentham Hall. Stone is also recorded as being removed in the 1680s. The cave was out of bounds during the Second World War when munitions were stored there. Others suggest that gold reserves were hidden there by the Bank of England when they moved to Trentham. Huge iron doors guarded the cave entrance.

The Long Bridge

This bridge is of medieval origin and was probably built by the canons of Trentham priory. In 1630 it consisted of five great arches and measured 360 feet, including its causeway. The bridge was allocated £200 for repairs and an upgrade in 1635. It was widened in 1703, and again in the 1840s to be used as a service road to the hall. The south abutment wall is original and the joints from widening are clear from below the bridge.

Richard Beasley

Richard Beasley, son of Richard Beasley of Pelsall and Elinor Potter of Tamworth, was known as Fat Dick. He died of dropsy and was buried on 30 January 1722 in Trentham churchyard, aged sixty-three. In the courtyard near the steps is a curious inscription. It reads, 'Here Pullo is laid, on purpose 'tis said, to wait on Fat Dick if he's able, when to cellar he's been, and filled up to ye brim, he'd wait on him to ye coach stable.' Pullo was a dog belonging to Richard Beasley, coachman to Earl Gower, who liked his ale.

New Trentham Hall

This 1829 engraving by Lacey shows the exterior of the neoclassical hall that was built around the core of the old hall to reflect the growing status of the Leveson Gower family. The drawing was sketched by artist John Preston Neal, who was a clerk at the general post office. He died at Tattingstone in November 1847. Park Brook Bridge (*below*) can be seen on his drawings. Artist John Constable painted Trentham Hall in the summer of 1801 when he stayed with his relations at Great Fenton.

The Mausoleum

Designed by Charles Tatham and built of ashlar stone for the second Marquis of Stafford in 1808 in an Egyptian style, the mausoleum emulates the Roman practice of being entombed beside the main highway. It is 40 feet square at the base and 40 feet high. The inside was of black polished marble with forty catacombs. It cost £5,068 12s to build. The Marquis was created Duke of Sutherland in 1833, but died shortly afterwards and was buried at Dornoch Cathedral, Sutherland.

Mausoleum Catacombs

These catacombs contained George Granville, the 2nd Duke, his wife, Duchess Harriet, their children Alexandrina, Albert, Blanche and Victoria, along with their grandson, George Granville. In 1892, the 3rd Duke George Granville William died and wished to be buried in the earth. In 1888, he had married his mistress following duchess Anne's death in London. The new duchess was buried nearby in 1912, but has no epitaph. In 1905, the 4th Duke Cromatie removed the contents of the catacombs and placed them beneath the earth, therein marked by catacomb stones.

Tittensor Monument

This monument features the figure
of the 1st duke, whose original was
only 4 feet tall and made for Dornoch
Cathedral. A giant copy was made
for Ben Brhaggie that overlooked
Dunrobin Castle by a journeyman of
Chantrey, named Joseph Theakstone.
Charles Wink's column design for
Tittensor was rejected because it
could be mistaken for a factory
chimney. The Tittensor figure was
sculpted by another pupil named
Grange in 1836. Chantrey's inspection
showed alarming deterioration and
he ordered gallons of linseed oil to be
applied. Contrary to guidebooks, it is
not made of bronze but stone.

OULTON ABBEY

Oulton Abbey

The abbey was purchased by John Joule, brewer, in 1822 and he remained there until 1835 when the 2nd Duke of Sutherland bought it to live in while Trentham Hall was being rebuilt. The duke resold it in 1838 to Mrs Sarah Bakewell, who made it a private lunatic asylum and renamed it Oulton Retreat. Thomas and Sarah Bakewell came from Spring Vale, Tittensor, where they had previously run an asylum for the well-to-do. Only the lodge remains, known as Wren's Nest Cottage.

TITTENSOR CHASE LODGE

Spring Vale

The vale has several freshwater springs and was known as 'Boxer's Parlour', where a woman of ill repute named Ruth Morris lived. The top spring rises at a place called Saxons Gullet. Spring Vale was called 'Fair Springs' until 1808, when Thomas Bakewell erected a board stating 'Spring Vale Asylum'. The old Waggersley Asylum was purchased in 1840 by the duke who built Tittensor Chase House nearby. In July 1914, Gresham Copeland obtained it for £18,900. Robert Copeland was born there in 1925.

CHASE HOUSE, TITTENSOR.

Trentham Hall

The hall was transformed into a ducal palace by James Trubshaw from Colwich, near Rugeley, where he is also buried. His descendant was Brian Trubshaw, test pilot for Concorde in 1969. The hall's construction began in 1834, and by 1840 the build was almost finished, at a cost of £150,000 – more than treble the original estimate. The H-shape of the 1633 house was incorporated into Charles Barry's design. Trentham had 200 rooms and put a heavy strain on the duke's coffers.

Trentham Festivities

Celebrations were held at Trentham in January 1850 to commemorate the coming of age of the Marquis of Stafford, the duke's eldest son. Preparations at Trentham were extensive, with fifty sheep and a score of fine oxen slaughtered. Several hogsheads of fine ale from the duke's cellars were broached. Flags were hoisted at Trentham Inn and triumphal arches of evergreen were erected over the entrance to the park and at Ash Green. Beef, bread and ale were distributed to the Trentham Estate cottagers.

Deer of the Estate

Benjamin Disraeli, the Earl of Beaconsfield, wrote *Lothair* in 1870, a thinly disguised story of Trentham, which he described as an Italian palace of freestone with a park of ferny solitudes where fallow deer trooped. Beyond the lake the scene became more savage, with the dark form of red deer on the high ground. Venison was regularly supplied to the Bishop of Lichfield, judges at Stafford Assizes and other persons of note. Red deer were eventually eaten to extinction in the region, but a small herd of black fallow deer still roam Trentham Woods.

Dog Kennel Lane

The lane was built in 1842 as the new direct route to Whitmore station. The 2nd Duke of Sutherland gave his eldest son permission to build kennels to house his spaniel gundogs. However, he was surprised at the scale and progress his son had made during his absence in 1845. The family were known dog breeders, notably mastiffs. The North Staffordshire hunting hounds relocated to Trentham in 1862 and the kennels were enlarged to include lodgings. In 1944, the Albion Greyhounds used the kennels. All have been demolished, except one cottage dated 1879.

Dairyfields

Dairyfields lay on the opposite side of the road, which was clearly marked in May 1929 as Kennels Road when the area was offered for sale as the finest building site in the district. It comprised over 27 acres, with the unique advantage of overlooking the sylvan beauties of Trentham Park. Dairy House itself was built in the early 1880s, but was enlarged after demolition of the hall to provide accommodation for visiting Leveson Gowers and home to Hugh Fraser MP during the 1945 parliamentary elections.

Hargreaves Lodge

Built in 1896, the lodge was designed by Thomas Roberts, surveyor for the Trentham Estate. It guarded the entrance to the hall from the north edge of Trentham Park. The drive ran through ancient woodland named Hargreaves Wood, which was sold by Trentham Park Golf Club in 2014 for £155,000. The drive passes over Park Brook via a balustraded bridge. References are made to a bridge that crossed Lancelot Brown's ha-ha west of Trentham Lake being removed to Park Brook.

Gravel Pit Lodge

The lodge was built in 1859, mainly to control the amount of gravel being taken from the quarry. It was designed by architect George Devey of London and has its construction date moulded into the rendering over the south-facing window. The present owner is in dispute with the authorities over the direction that the building work should take with regard to the date plaque. Until then, the scaffolding remains in situ.

The Gravel Pit at Hanchurch Quarries

The gravel pit was used to supply gravel for the paths around Trentham Hall as well as for building purposes over a longer period of time. The pit also supplied other landed gentry's projects, and in the 1840s there was concern over the amount of gravel being excavated. In 1935, Trentham Gravel Ltd advertised that the works supplied aggregate and ferro sand. The quarry fell out of use until the arrival of the motorway, when, in 1961, John Laing proposed removing the whole escarpment.

The M6 Motorway

When the M6 arrived in 1961, it wound a brown ribbon through Trentham with round-the-clock construction undertaken by contractor John Laing. A culvert 25 feet below the road was built to take water from Hanchurch pools. In addition, the main cable for the Independent Television Authorities had to be accommodated beneath the Eccleshall Road bridge footings. The bridge from the gravel pit lodge led to a carriage drive that led on to the hall lined with elm and lime trees, now fenced off because juveniles were launching projectiles on to the traffic.

Trumpet-Shaped Junction

This junction at Hanchurch took three months to design and was opened to traffic in November 1963. A diversion was built in the woods opposite Eddie Stobart to allow its construction. The motorway had no crash barriers, speed limits or lights. Sections prone to fog had lights placed at 1-mile intervals worked by a car battery that was switched on with a key by a police patrolman. There was a thirty-car pile-up on Bonfire Night in 1965 and an immediate speed limit was introduced.

Trentham Estate's Boundary Wall

The wall was built around the Trentham Estate to keep poachers out. Between 1765 and 1767, John Ansley was paid £150 to provide 300,000 bricks, while Edward and John Shaw were paid £200 to take down and rebuild the park wall to a height of 6 feet, topped by stone coping on the south and west wall. Much of the wall remains at Tittensor and the west of the estate, towards Toft Farm, which has been cut off by the motorway.

Trentham Inn

The inn was originally named The Goats Head, probably due to the goats' heads that adorned the gates of Trentham Hall, which were added in 1633. The inn was rebuilt in 1777 on the east side of the Stone Road, now Trentham Gardens Close. The above business card is from 1833 for the innkeeper, Nathaniel Crisp, who died in 1838. Crisp was a friend of James Caldwell and they experimented with Wedgwood on enamel colours. Nathaniel's widow, Charlotte, married John Swift from Blurton and the inn changed name to Sutherland Arms. It closed in 1867.

The West Entrance to Trentham Hall

This entrance is perhaps the most impressive of the hall's remains. It was approached by a goose-foot pattern of drives that led to the duke's other properties at Tittensor, Newcastle and Lilleshall. The semi-circular corridors leading from the porte cochère went to the library and private apartments to the right and the grand staircase and guest rooms to the left. The two lodges were designed by Charles Heathcote Tatham and were moved to Stone Road, facing the mausoleum, in 1938.

The Golden Gates at Trentham Hall

These intricate gates are gilded replicas of those at Buckingham Palace, possibly made at Coalbrookdale, Shropshire, near the duke's Lilleshall Estate. They were removed from Trentham's grand entrance and installed at Lilleshall Hall, with the date 1895 fixed into the wrought-iron scrollwork that still has the duke's coronet at its apex. They were taken down for renovation in 2008 and rehung, but are no longer used. They are Grade II listed.

Porte Cochère at Trentham Hall

This covered entrance was built to impress and is constructed from solid stone, unlike most of the hall which is brick stucco. Above three sides are the heavily worked arms of the 2nd duke. A Scottish wildcat at the top stands for the Earls of Sutherland, with stylised wolf supporters known as gores. Three laurel leafs for Leveson and a single cross on banded background for Gower have been inscribed. The motto translates as 'You may break but will never bend me'. The duke's coronet sits at the top.

The Private Conservatory

The conservatory was one of the gems of Trentham, a miniature world of flowers with eleven Italian windows to match Charles Tatham's orangery arches. It had trellised walls with a trellised ceiling between the many lights that hung there. A figure of Venus bathing stood in a small pool surrounded by exotic plants and ferns. The engraving is copied from a photograph by Harrison. A twin wing that projected to the east contained the dining room, and its windows were purchased during demolition by Hamlet Embrey for use at Embrey's Bakery, Fenton.

West Court

West Court was a private paved area with flower beds and a shell fountain with Venus rising from the bath at its centre. There were doors separating it from the hall that could be removed to incorporate the area into a special room for large occasions, such as the duke's eldest son's coming of age in 1850. The above photograph is dated 1933 and it appears that the shell fountain has been removed. Today's image shows the serious deterioration that has taken place since.

Bowling Alley

The alley was created by the 3rd Duke of Sutherland in the former orangery arcade. The Shah of Persia was a guest in 1873. The shah asked if the duke bowled and the duke and several noblemen immediately stripped off their hats and coats to proceed in the game. The Prince of Wales was so impressed during his visit that he built a bowling alley at Sandringham. The arcade was taken over by artist Fred England in 1995 as a gallery.

The Orangery

The orangery was designed by Charles Heathcote Tatham in 1808, who also designed the mausoleum and the twin entrance lodges that now face it. In an alcove at the orangery was a bust of the 1st Duke of Sutherland, which is said to have been placed in the church, but seems a different design. Tatham also built a conservatory, which stood on the site later used by Charles Barry for his conservatory. In 1804, he designed a greenhouse in the style of an Egyptian temple, but this was not used.

George Fleming, Head Gardener at Trentham Hall

George Fleming was born in Sutherland in 1809. He was a gardener at Lilleshall Hall before becoming head gardener at Trentham Hall in 1841. After William Nesfield had completed the water features, the task of laying flowerbeds fell to Fleming. He planted many rhododendrons and introduced ribbon planting. He was promoted to land steward in 1860 and died in 1876 at Hanchurch. He is buried beneath a large tree that faces the window of the mausoleum with a white tabletop tomb.

Zadock Stevens

Zadock Stevens was born in
Spondon in 1832 and lodged at
the bothy in 1861 when Archibald
Henderson took over from Fleming.
Henderson moved to Croydon
and Zadock was made head
gardener. He invested in Brazilian
sugar, Russian stock and Madras'
railways. He died in October 1886,
and is buried beneath a large
polished-granite stone at the corner
of the mausoleum. His German-born
wife died of belladonna poisoning
in 1887 after having been given
the incorrect medicine bottle by
her daughter.

Peter Christie Blair

Peter Christie Blair was born in 1855 at Largo, the same birthplace as Alexander Selkirk (the inspiration for *Robinson Crusoe*). In 1881, he was in lodgings at Kings Road, Fulham. He took over from Zadock Stevens and became the last head gardener. After the Boer War, seventy gardeners were dismissed and Blair was living among the ruins of the famous glasshouses of Trentham in the gardener's house. Blair died in June 1937 at 'Hobart', his house in Lindum Avenue, and was buried at Trentham.

Head Gardener's House, Trentham Hall

The head gardener's house was designed by Charles Barry for George Fleming. In 1847, Fleming had forty-three gardeners, five labourers and seven plantation workers under him. The house stood in the kitchen gardens, which had stone arches running south to protect the plants yet still allowed access. However, only one arch remains. The gardens were established in 1743 by specialist David Patton of Chiswick. The west wall of the kitchen gardens was removed and replaced by a long conservatory with arches that then became the ballroom.

Children's Cottage

This cottage was built in 1840 for the 2nd duke's children, a few yards away from the head gardener's house on the other side of Longton brook, with a play area at the front. It was altered in 1890 by Thomas Roberts, architect for the duke. Like most of the remains of Trentham Hall, it is Grade II listed. It was later used as part of the bothy, which still stands next door to the cottage, to house young gardeners and keep them away from the hall housemaids.

Tulip Poplar

This must be one of the earliest trees to have been planted in the pleasure gardens. *Lidiodendron tulipfera*, yellow poplar, was introduced from the eastern United States in 1688, the tallest eastern hardwood that is fast-growing in moist soil. It is known as the 'canoe wood' tree by Native Americans and is favoured for building log cabins. Becoming rare in the wild, this particular specimen loves its position beside the river, but is in constant danger of toppling into the Trent, despite careful pruning.

Iron Bridge

The remains of this bridge can be seen beneath the bridge that was built in 1931 by Arches restaurant. The iron bridge, built in 1794, was replaced in 1890. Despite its proud boast of being the world's second iron bridge after Ironbridge Gorge, another cast-iron bridge was built at Kirklees Park, Yorkshire, in 1769, along with others in the same county. Trentham's iron bridge was made at Coalbrookdale and cost £900, with stone abutments quarried at Salt. It replaced an earlier stone one that had stood downriver.

River Trent Footbridge

This bridge was built further south over the Trent to connect the pleasure gardens to the growing beds. Erected in 1893, it was a 70-foot suspension bridge with tubular cast-iron pylons. It was light, graceful in outline and strong. The anchorages served both the cables and deck. It was made by Louis Harper at Craiginches Works, Aberdeen. Today's bridge (*pictured*) seems feeble in comparison, but the new steel bridge at the garden's entrance lifts the spirit.

Floodgate Cottage

The cottage was built around 1858 at the south end of the lake. Probably designed by George Devey, an architect from London who had worked extensively for the Duke of Sutherland at Cliveden and Trentham. Devey never married and died at Hastings in 1886. Floodgate was useful in controlling trespassers, but its main function was to control the sluice gates, which had to be opened when the lake needed to be drained, so as to remove silt washed down by the Trent.

The Cascade

The cascade was built by canal engineer James Brindley, who was introduced to Lord Stafford by the Earl's agent, John Gilbert, from Cotton, near Alton Towers. From this work, Brindley went on to build the Bridgewater Canal in 1759. The purpose of the cascade was to form a picturesque way of removing surplus water when the river flooded. It has fourteen steps and there is a smaller cascade of five steps where park brook joins the Trent.

Pickford Lodges

The lodges were built in 1776, chosen from several designs by Joseph Pickford of Derby who had completed work for Josiah Wedgwood. They guarded the old London Road drive from Tittensor to Trentham Hall and were later extended by Trentham surveyor Thomas Roberts. The first inhabitant was park keeper James Penson, whose family had served the Levesons since 1580. The lodges still stand and are now the entrance to Trentham Monkey Forest.

Tittensor Lodge

The lodge was built in 1823 as the new entrance to Trentham Hall, after the old London Road towards Monument Lane at Tittensor became built up and congested. It stood in the middle of the dual carriageway, about halfway between the new roundabout at Monkey Forest and the first cottage at Tittensor. It was demolished in 1961 when Stone Road became a dual carriageway. In 1893, a new triangular milepost was erected outside, which stands uselessly on the central reservation.

The Lodge, Tittensor

Mileposts

These were introduced by the Romans, and stone mileposts had to be erected by law along the Talke–Trentham Road when it was turnpiked in 1714 and then extended to Tittensor for Lord Gower. In 1893 Charles Lathe of Tipton had an order for 335 triangular iron replacements. Two survivors stand on the central reservation on Stone Road, with a further two on Longton Road to Blurton and a single survivor near Hargreaves Lodge Whitmore Road.

Spring Valley

The stream was fed by a spring that rises at Black Lake, near Toft Farm, described in 1857 as 'a beautiful dell with crystal clear water'. It was a favourite spot with day-trippers who regularly broke down fences to reach their goal. Three footbridges crossed the stream, one of which is now inside the Monkey Forest's perimeter fence. The ice-cold water fed the open-air swimming pool and can still be traced trickling into Trentham Lake.

Outdoor Swimming Pool

The pool was opened in July 1935 and was very popular with visitors. In was built in Art-Deco style with a clock that had fish-shaped hands, more in keeping with Hollywood than Trentham. In 1964, it was a scene of tragedy when Shrewsbury Town goalkeeper Paul Mellor died from choking on his food after diving into the pool. He is buried at Gnosall. The pool closed in 1974 due to mining subsidence and was demolished in 1986, with all buildings bulldozed into the pool.

Miniature Railway

The railway had three petrol-driven engines named *Dunrobin* No. 1769, *Brora* No. 1695 and *Golspie* No. 2085. *Brora* and *Dunrobin* were made for Lilleshall Hall pleasure grounds in 1929 and were used until they were put into storage during the war. They were moved to Trentham and joined the new engine *Golspie* from 1934 onwards, until they went to Alton Towers. *Golspie* is waiting refurbishment at Amerton Farm, *Brora* is on display at Dunrobin station while *Dunrobin* is in use at Tilford in Surrey.

Lakeside Chalet

The chalet was built in the Swiss style in 1934 and was the terminus for the miniature railway, supplying teas, ice cream and snacks. The chalet is still open for business eighty years later. The building has hardly changed, apart from a frontage added to give customers shelter. If you look carefully along the path approaching beside the lake, you may spot pieces of railway track sticking up, indicating that the rails were never removed.

Paddle Boats

Paddle boats have been on the lake since 1930. The postcard shows two of them in 1950. One was called *Lousiannah Bell*, a forty-seater that fell out of use and was moored in 1985. She was sent for repair to Nottingham in 1989. Near the stables is the remains of a paddle boat that was used as a reed cutter before being grounded and filled with flower displays. Today's cruiser is a forty-two-seat, battery-operated catamaran named *Miss Elizabeth*.

Triple Georgian Boathouse

The boathouse was probably built around 1760 when the lake was enlarged by Lancelot Brown and has downward steps at the rear. It's nice to speculate that it once housed a gondola that was used on the lake. An 1840 boathouse was incorporated into the dam, which stopped the Trent flooding the gardens. The ruined paddle boat near the stables lay embedded in mud at this later boathouse for years.

Rose Walk

The cast-iron rose walk trellis was designed by George Fleming in 1847 and is 100 m long. It stands on top of the dam and was covered in roses to protect the ladies' complexion as they promenaded. Six S-shaped cast-iron support scrolls were discovered at Taylor Casting, Cobridge, in 2012. They had been made for Trentham but were never collected. They were eagerly snapped up by Trentham Estate and proudly fixed into place.

Rose Garden

In 1857, the rose garden was known as the parterre garden, with a path around the edge and divided into quarters. In the middle was a circular bed divided into eight segments, with a bronze statue of a lightly draped lady leaning back onto a pedestal decorated with aquatic motifs at the centre and known locally as the 'lady of the sea'. She was thought to be a copy and Grade II listed in 1984. An ugly modern building to the left was a go-cart arena.

Perseus

Perseus was made in Florence in 1549 by Benvenuto Cellini and is on display at Loggia Dei Lonzi. It belonged to the Duke of Tuscany, who allowed his friend, the 2nd Duke of Sutherland, to make a copy in 1847. It was removed to Sutton Place in 1918, but returned to Trentham in 1966 by the Countess of Sutherland. During its absence, a sundial and a statue of a French lady were displayed. It was cleaned in 2012 when it was taken to the Royal Academy exhibition.

Frozen Lake, Trentham
The frost at Trentham was very severe in March 1895 and woodsmen took advantage of a shortcut using carts across the lake. James Edwards, pictured with a beard outside his Cocknage Wood home, went onto the lake to assist and plunged through the ice. He was rescued but died of enteric fever from effluence in the lake on 6 March and was buried at Blurton. The skaters were photographed near *Perseus* in February 1912, shortly before demolition of the hall in May. (*Image courtesy of Newcastle Borough Museum*)

Icehouse

The icehouse was built into the side of an old quarry in 1843 on Park Drive and was described as an ice well on drawing plans. Its purpose was to store meat from the nearby slaughterhouse, with ice collected from the lake insulated with straw. A Georgian icehouse of 1760 has been discovered by workers on the west side of the lake, but little remains above ground. Trentham Estate plans to excavate the remains.

Demolition of Trentham Hall

The demolition started in May 1912, partly because of pollution in the lake and partly to reduce the duke's expenditure. The sale of doors and windows took place in September 1911, everything going for a fraction of its actual cost. The Belvedere Tower failed to find a buyer, but was eventually snapped up by the Sandon Estate and rebuilt in a field. Another tower from the stable court was used at the rebuilding of Biddulph Grange by Thomas Bower.

Secret Tunnels

Underground secretive passages abound at Trentham, where the domestic staff appear to have spent most of their time. The passageway pictured runs beneath the porte cochère and was where Richard Beasley supped his ale. The thickness of its walls suggest it was once part of the priory. The bricked-up archway leads to a set of steps that came out in the servants' hall – who knows what secrets it holds? A recent exploration has found passages blocked up by modern brickwork.

FIRE
HYDRANT
20 FEET

Richard Leveson

Richard Leveson was a privateer who died in August 1605. His corpse was embalmed and conveyed to Saint Peter's, Wolverhampton. A huge gunmetal monument by Hubert Le Suer was erected to him, which was vandalised by Cromwell's soldiers. Only this figure, in admiral's uniform, was rescued and hidden at Lilleshall until the restoration of the monarchy and returned to Wolverhampton. The stone figure in the alcove of the clock tower at Trentham is a copy. Sir Richard was interred at Wolverhampton.

The Clock Tower

The clock tower was built to remind estate workers of the time using a bell chime. On its pinnacle stood a copy of a bronze figure of Genius of Liberty, purchased in Paris by the 2nd Duke in 1837. It was cut into sections and fitted with iron to strengthen its lofty position and installed in 1846 at Trentham. It was still there during demolition in 1912, but disappeared and was only rediscovered in a private collection in America in 2012. A copy was made for Cliveden in 1861.

Sculpture Gallery

The sculpture gallery was left standing after demolition of the hall because it was being used as workshops by Duchess Millicent's Cripples' Guild. One central building was demolished to allow access to the new bridge over the Trent to the kitchen gardens, which had replaced a ferry boat worked by pulling on a rope. Beneath the clock tower was the entrance to the dairy with the inscription *'Lac Non Defit'*, which translates to 'Milk Does Not Fail'. The gallery was used as a temporary church in 1844.

Horse Graves

These horse graves are marked by large sandstone blocks and beneath an old cedar tree. The inscriptions are very worn, but the names Sunbeam Shah and Dolly can be made out. Dolly was Duke Cromartie's shooting pony and died aged twelve. The horse stables have survived, but the building that stood in the centre of the stable yard, containing footmen's recreations rooms and other stables with a hayloft, have been removed and is used as a storage yard at present.

Bandstand

The bandstand's remains can be found stored in dense undergrowth behind the stables. It once stood just north of the rose arch. Brass bands were a popular event at Trentham and in 1925 Willenhall, Shelton, Pendleton and Shelton Iron & Steel brass bands performed there. Some photographs were taken of the bandstand in 1989 before its removal to the naughty corner behind the stables. Unwanted fridge-freezers look on in disgust from the stables' archway.

The Chairlift

The chairlift was another popular attraction that took day-trippers from the gardens to the top of Jacob's Ladder, at a gradient of one in seven. It was opened on 6 July 1965 by Trentham entertainment's manager Geraldo and operated by a company from Uttoxeter. On a windy day soon after opening, the mechanism failed and firemen with ladders and rope had to rescue people stranded high in the air. The ride was closed but remains can be found among the ferns.

Elephant Clump

Elephant Clump was a group of beech trees that stood on the high ridge above Trentham Park and resembled an elephant when viewed from Shelton. They were described by some as the seven sisters, but, as can been seen, there were only five trees. They were removed in 1976 and a replacement tree was planted in 1977 by Cauldon College Students Union and Trentham Estate. The ridge was part of the king's hunting forest and ancient oaks record its history.

Trentham's Fences

Fences were always contentious in Trentham's woods. In 1201, the canons of Trentham priory were granted permission to erect a fence, provided it did not hinder free passage of King John's deer. The dukes of Sutherland allowed access to the woods beyond the fence only on certain days, but, as usual, people took advantage and did damage to trees and fences. The caravan park at Trentham was very popular, seen just beyond the fencepost.

The Service Entrance to the Estate Yard

This entrance is over a bridge, which was originally a drawbridge over Richard Leveson's moat that had surrounded the hall. The tall building to the left was the estate office, whose windows allowed observance of all goods in and out of the yard. The ancient elm beside the bridge is now reduced to a stump. The lodge behind had a drinking fountain in the wall with three cups. Both lodge and fountain are no more and the estate office sits with broken windows, awaiting its fate.

Loggias

Loggias were built in the gardens at Trentham, with two having a three-bay design to provide shelter east and west of the hall and another set of one-bay design to house statues in mirror positions near the hall. Only one three-bay loggia remains, its twin taken to Lilleshall in 1898 while a single-arch loggia was moved in 1913 to be placed at the centre of the private Sutherland burial ground at Dunrobin, overlooking the Dornoch Firth where Duke Cromartie was the first interment.

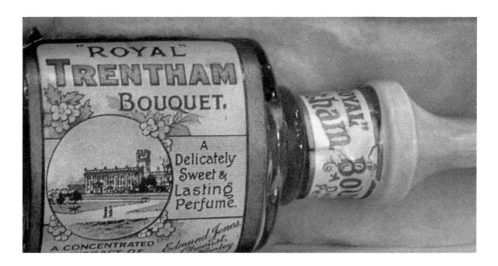

Trentham Bouquet Perfume

This perfume was described by Millicent Duchess of Sutherland as 'sweet and lasting'. Produced by Edmund Jones, chemist, at his premises on Miles Bank, Hanley, he provided samples to the Princess of Wales and Princess Victoria, who then placed orders from Sandringham. Eddy's Royal Trentham Bouquet was ordered to perfume the balconies and mayor's parlour at the Victoria Hall in 1897 during the royal visit. Clara Butt and Ellen Terry were both regular customers.

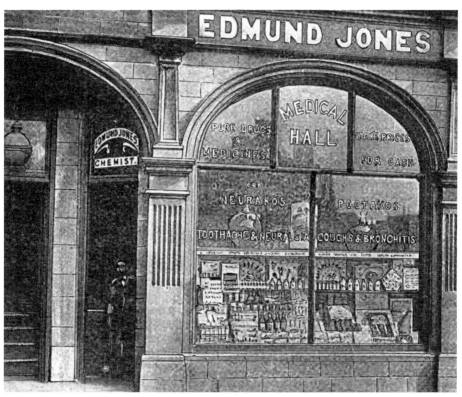

The Blacksmith's Shop on Park Drive
The blacksmith's shop is a peculiar triangular-shaped building with a tiny yard at the back. Originally built without a door, it had an open grill fixed into the horseshoe-shaped front and a large, round, segmented grill window at the rear. Flame shapes made from copper stood at the top of the pillars and must have been impressive in the sunlight. The last blacksmith to work here was Abraham Clay who, in 1912, lived at Ash Green.

The Threat of Fire

Fire was always a worry for the owners of the estate, due to the legion of candles that illuminated the hall. The duke had two Shand Mason horse-drawn steam fire engines that took ten minutes to pick up steam on the way to the fire. He had his own fire brigade at the hall. In 1876, he gave a demonstration by shooting a jet of water over the top of the stable yard clock tower. Around the hall itself were strategically placed leather fire buckets emblazoned with a Sutherland badge in polychrome and gilt.

The Fire Engine House

The fire engine house and cart shed were on the yard alongside the blacksmith's shop on Park Drive, which led through an arch to Home Farm quadrangle. On a hill overlooking the yard was the surveyor's house, home to Thomas Roberts, architect to the Trentham Estate from late 1840 until he retired to Robin Hood's Bay, Yorkshire, aged eighty-one. The house had one room fitted out with wooden pigeonholes to store maps and plans. It was renamed Elelme and is now a private residence.

The Gas House

The gas house was built in an old quarry on Park Drive, complete with gasholder. The owners employed a man named Elijah Derbyshire from Worsley, Lancashire, to produce coal gas to light the newly built hall. In 1862, he was moved to operate a new gasworks for the duke at Golspie, Sutherland. The duke complained that more coal was being used to produce the same amount of gas. Elijah explained that the coal was poor quality compared with that originating from Staffordshire.

Duchess's Girls' School

The school was opened in a pair of converted cottages around 1840. The school occupied one cottage while the schoolmistress lived in the other. The girls received a new hat and cloak every other year. To save expenditure in 1863, the school was moved to one of the cottages near the old bridge over the Trent. The North Staffordshire Hunt took over the original girls' school before they moved to Hill Chorlton in 1930. The old school became private residences.

Turbine Farm

The turbine farm had sluice gates to control the river and two water turbines below ground driving Crompton generators that produced a 50V direct current, suitable only for lighting, connected to the hall by thick copper wires in a trench. Power was maintained by large glass accumulator batteries upstairs over the turbine pits, with a manual switch at turbine farm. The sluice gates were removed in 1940 and the turbine pits were rediscovered when new car inspection pits were dug.

Cottage Ruins

These ruins stand by the medieval bridge on Park Drive. These four cottages replaced an earlier cottage that was demolished in 1842 as part of the duke's improvement scheme. A piper named Macbeth was the first inhabitant with Robert Wright, village baker, next door and a stud groom named Topping in the end cottage. The middle cottage became a Sunday school. The cottages were abandoned twenty-five years ago and are up for sale with a price tag of over £300,000.

Leisure Garden Entrance

This entrance was created when the two limestone lodges, designed by Tatham, were moved from the west entrance of the hall in 1938. They were just large enough to have one room inside. This new entrance used to be a private road that was used by the family to take the deceased to the mausoleum opposite. The lodges were mounted with a bronze buck and doe deer, but these were sold. Trentham Garden's sign lies hidden in the trees.

The Ballroom

The ballroom was built in 1931 on the site of the old kitchen gardens and incorporated the arches of Fleming's conservatory. In 1938, balconies and a new concrete bridge over the Trent into the gardens were added. The first resident bandleader was named Al and he was a nephew of a Jewish emigrant named Israel Isidore Beilin, who might be better known as Irving Berlin. The ballroom was a popular venue and hosted many famous names until it closed and was demolished in 2002.

London Clearing Banks

These banks were moved to Trentham during the war to be saved from the damage caused by the Blitz. A monument in the shape of a 50p piece was placed on a plinth, which originally boasted a sculpture that was then replaced by a small flower pedestal. The banker's monument in bronzed fibreglass is by sculptor Robert Berkoff and was unveiled by the Countess of Sutherland in 1976. It was refurbished in December 1995. The sculpture has emblems of all the clearing banks around its rim.

The Schoolmaster's House

The house was home to headteacher Claude Ramon Forse, killed in military action in 1918. His wife, Margaret, was also a teacher who died in 1973, aged ninety-three. Claude is one of seventeen names on Trentham War Memorial of Darley Dale stone, a gift of the women of Trentham, unveiled in October 1921. The building with the bell turret in the distance was the Trentham Institute, built on the site of Trentham Inn. New houses occupy the schoolhouse site.

Ash Green, Trentham.

Ash Green and Trentham Villages

These villages have both expanded through time and can no longer be separated. Here and there glimpses of the past can be stumbled upon, such as West View, which hides from the modern world behind greenery. It must be one of the oldest houses in Trentham and sits just yards away from the brash new roundabout, which is the entrance to Trentham Estate. In 1912, it was home to James Underhill.

The Kitchen Garden Wall to Trentham Hall

This wall can be seen behind the horse and cart. The tree in the centre is where Thomas Brookfield, owner of Brookfields Hardware, Trentham Road, hit his head falling from his bicycle and died in November 1915. The thatched cottage behind the lady was the post office and was demolished to be replaced by Ash Green garage, whose cars can be seen displayed below. The other half of the cottage still stands but is unrecognisable.

COTTAGES AT TRENTHAM.

Thatched Cottages

Thatched cottages were a feature of Trentham that were gradually replaced by the Duke of Sutherland due to the risk of fire. Thankfully some remain. A terraced row named Ivy Cottages has recently been re-thatched for the second time in thirty years, but the other terraced row (*pictured*) were demolished to make way for an Amoco filling station, now Fast Lane motor showroom. The cottage on the end was a shop with a sign saying 'Licensed to sell tobacco'.

Peacock House, Park Drive
Peacock House was home to Simon Fielding, who was an authority on dogs and poultry and worked for the duke. He invested in a pottery. His son, Abraham Fielding, had to bail out his father's Railway Pottery and renamed it Crown Devon. Abraham and his brother-in-law, Taylor, built large houses on Longton Road near the old police station that is now NatWest Bank. Fielding was a member of the North Staffordshire Hunt and had plates made featuring hunt dogs named Trentham Sandstorm and Champion Cosy (*pictured*).

Conservatory
Trentham Gardens. 6.

Glasshouses at Trentham Kitchen Gardens

These glasshouses were 600 yards long and known as the Trentham Glass Case. They stretched the entire length of the new Blue Diamond garden centre, all the way to the arches that still stand. The garden walls had cavities that were heated with urn-shaped flues along the top, a design named Trentham Wall Case. Fresh flowers were taken every day to Trentham station and sent to the Duchess at Stafford House, London.

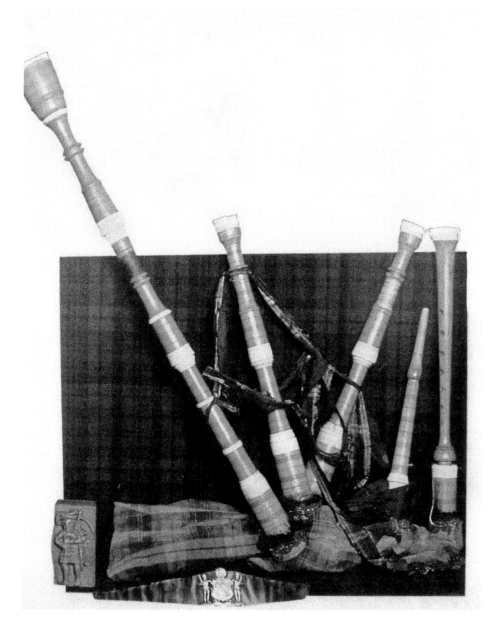

Scottish Pipes

Scottish pipes became a feature of Trentham when the 1st Duke married the Countess of Sutherland. On his death in 1836, a monument was raised at Tittensor with a piper named George Clark employed to guard it in full Highland dress while the family were in residence. John Macbeth from Dunrobin became the next piper to the duke, until he left in 1850 to manage an inn called The Haunch of Venison at New Bond Street, London. The family moved to Newport, Monmouthshire, where he died in 1852. John Macalister was the next piper from Sutherland, who faithfully served the duke for forty-six years until his death 1886. He is buried to the rear of the mausoleum with a large grey granite slab. Macalister's pipes date from the time of the Battle of Culloden and are displayed at Dunrobin Castle.

Stoke-on-Trent Pubs

Mervyn Edwards

Filled with interesting trivia on the pubs and landlords of the
Potteries, author Mervyn Edwards takes you on a tour of the most
historic alehouses in Stoke-on-Trent.

978 1 4456 3943 7
96 pages, full colour